THE 10

Most Unforgettable Shipwrecks

Anita Griffith

Series Editor
Jeffrey D. Wilhelm

Much thought, debate, and research went into choosing and ranking the 10 items in each book in this series. We realize that everyone has his or her own opinion of what is most significant, revolutionary, amazing, deadly, and so on. As you read, you may agree with our choices, or you may be surprised — and that's the way it should be!

Franklin Watts®
an imprint of
SCHOLASTIC

www.scholastic.com/librarypublishing

A Rubicon book published in association with Scholastic Inc.

Rubicon © 2007 Rubicon Publishing Inc.
www.rubiconpublishing.com

Associate Publishers: Kim Koh, Miriam Bardswich
Project Editor: Amy Land
Editor: Christine Boocock
Editorial Assistant: Nikki Yeh
Senior Designer: Jeanette MacLean
Graphic Designer: Doug Baines

The publisher gratefully acknowledges the following for permission to reprint copyrighted material in this book.

Every reasonable effort has been made to trace the owners of copyrighted material and to make due acknowledgment. Any errors or omissions drawn to our attention will be gladly rectified in future editions.

"Medusa Expedition" from "The Medusa Shipwreck," November 7, 2006. Courtesy of Charles Mazel, Expedition Technical Director.

"Indepth: Climate Change." CBC News Online. March 24, 2005. Source: CBC.ca

"Churchill Tells Dramatic Story of Chase by Air and Sea." *Toronto Star*. May 27, 1941. Permission granted by Torstar Syndication Services.

"Underwater Explorer; Interview with Dr. Robert Ballard, President of the Institute for Exploration." Copyright © 1997 WGBH Educational Foundation. Website: http://www.pbs.org/wgbh/nova/titanic/ballard.html

Cover: Getty Images/The Image Bank/Max Dannenbaum

Library and Archives Canada Cataloguing in Publication

Griffith, Anita
    The 10 most unforgettable shipwrecks / Anita Griffith.

  Includes index.
ISBN 978-1-55448458-4

    1. Readers (Elementary) 2. Readers--Shipwrecks. I. Title.
II. Title: Ten most unforgettable shipwrecks.

PE1117.G77 2007   428.6   C2007-900551-9

2 3 4 5 6 7 8 9 10 11   10   20 19 18 17 16 15 14 13 12 11

Printed in Singapore

Contents

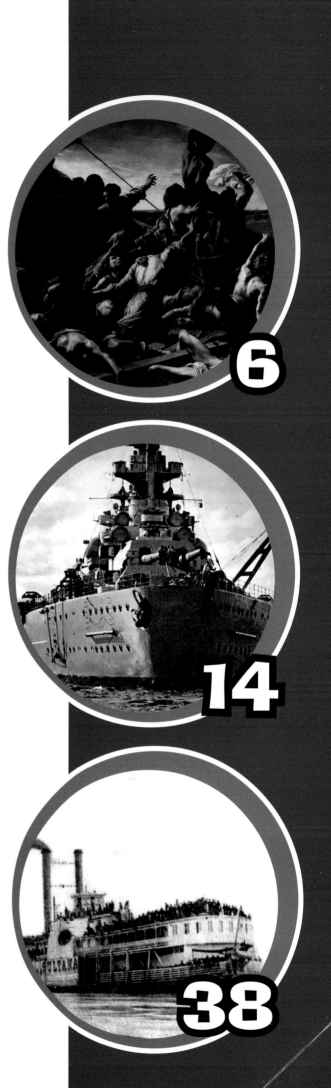

6

14

38

LOST SHIPS

Picture yourself sunbathing on the deck of the latest fully equipped cruise ship. Suddenly a deafening alarm sounds. The ship could be sinking, but you don't panic. Thanks to several safety drills, you know exactly what to do. Unfortunately, traveling the high seas wasn't always this safe …

In the past, sailing was often associated with excitement and adventure, but there were also real dangers. Ships were not built the way they are today, conditions on board were harsh, and there were few shipping rules or regulations. Plus, piracy and shipwrecks were a real threat!

The selections in this book are our pick of the 10 most unforgettable shipwrecks. Join us to explore the locations of these lost ships, the circumstances in which the ships went down, the tragic losses, and the impact of the disasters on us today. Think like a geographer or marine archeologist as we embark on our underwater adventure.

WHAT MAKES A SHIPWRECK UNFORGETTABLE?

(10) MEDUSA

How would you survive on a raft for 13 days without fresh water or food? When this happened to the crew of the frigate *Medusa*, they turned to cannibalism — eating human flesh — to stay alive.

This gruesome story began in June 1816 when four French ships set sail for Senegal, Africa. The captain of the *Medusa* picked up speed and sailed away from the other three ships. He got into trouble at the Arguin Bank, a large swampy area off the coast of Mauritania, West Africa. He sailed too close to the shoreline and his ship got stuck in the shallow water and mud.

A captain's supposed to go down with the ship. But, this one abandoned his after it started to break up. He and the passengers got onto lifeboats. Seventeen men chose to stay on the *Medusa*, and 150 crew members packed onto a makeshift raft. The plan was to have the lifeboats tow the raft to shore, but this didn't work and the raft was cut loose. When it was found 13 days later, only 15 men were alive!

makeshift: *temporary*

TYPE OF SHIP: A French frigate — a high-speed, medium-sized sailing war vessel

DATE OF SHIPWRECK: July 1816

WHAT'S UNUSUAL: The ship ran aground and its crew survived on a raft by turning to cannibalism.

This painting, Raft of the Medusa, *by Theodore Gericault (1791 – 1824), tells the grim story of the wreck.*

MEDUSA

WHERE IN THE WORLD?

The Arguin Bank, off the coast of Mauritania, is an area of mudflats, sand, and swamps. The water here is too shallow for large ships. They usually sail far out into the Atlantic Ocean, letting the current carry them south of the bank and away from shore.

THAT SINKING FEELING ...

After the *Medusa* ran aground, the water level was too low for the ship to get out of the mud. The crew tried to raise the ship by throwing cargo overboard, but they could not raise it high enough. Finally, when the hull broke in two and began filling with water, the captain decided to leave the ship.

hull: *body of a ship*

Quick Fact

The area around the Arguin Bank is home to a rich variety of fish, migrating birds, and unusual species of sea turtles and dolphins. It has been a UNESCO World Heritage site since 1989, and is called Arguin Bank National Park. This protected area extends 37 miles out into the ocean and 22 miles inland into the Sahara desert.

WHAT'S DOWN THERE?

The ship never sank — it was grounded deep in the mud. Thirteen days after the wreck, a rescue ship found the raft with human remains and only 15 survivors. The *Medusa* was found 54 days later, with only three sailors alive. The ship was supposed to be carrying gold, but this was never found. The rest of the wreck was discovered in 1980 by a French marine archeological expedition. They also found artifacts that identified the ship.

? Some people think of shipwrecks as gravesites that should not be disturbed. What are your feelings?

IMPACT

The story of the *Medusa* and her raft shocked Europe and almost brought down the French government. People were horrified by the captain's inexperience, the mistakes of the crew, the weak rescue effort, and the story of cannibalism. They were angry that the captain had survived on the lifeboat and failed to save the lives of his crew.

? What circumstances could justify cannibalism? Give your reasons.

Arguin Bank National Park in West Africa

Western Sahara (Occupied by Morocco)

West Africa

F'derik
Nouadhibou
Atar
Akjoujt
Mauritania
Tidjikja
Nouakchott
Saint-Louis
Aleg
Kiffa
Aioun el Atrouss
Tombouctou
Louga
Kaedi
Dakar
Diourbel
Mbour
Kaolack
Kayes
Banjul
Tambacounda
Mopti
Gambia
Mansa Konko
Kolda
Segou
Ouahigouya
Bamako
Nouna
Bissau
Dedougou

ALL-IMAGES–SHUTTERSTOCK

The Expert Says...

" The Arguin Bank, where the vessel ran aground, was a well-known danger common to every maritime map. "

— Erik Emptaz, author of *The Curse of the Medusa*

10   9   8   7   6

MEDUSA EXPEDITION

Dr. Charles Mazel is an ocean engineer and marine biologist, with extensive experience in underwater search and survey projects. He was the technical director of the French expedition that discovered the *Medusa* wreck in 1980. In this e-mail, dated November 2006, he describes what he found at the site of the wreck.

 Re: The *Medusa* Shipwreck

Thank you for your inquiry about the *Medusa* project. That took place in 1980, and I have no idea whatsoever about the current state of the wreck. I don't know if anyone's been out there in 20 years or more. What was there even when we did the project was buried in the sand, not sticking up prominently.

A variety of objects were recovered at the time we found the wreck. The most important are the ones that help in conclusively dating/identifying the wreck. Things as impressive as cannons with their makers' marks on them, and as simple as the copper spikes that held the ship together, but that had foundry marks on them that matched the foundry where it was known the *Medusa's* spikes were made. Interestingly, the history of the wreck said that they moved the cannons together on deck to try to help shift the weight to free the ship after it ran aground, and we found the cannons on the bottom heaped in a pile, so that made sense.

Also pottery, swords, bottles, pewter, and more — all the kinds of things you would expect to be on a ship. Enough was recovered to mount an exhibition at the Marine Museum in Paris not long after the project.

Hope this helps. Don't hesitate to ask if you have other questions.

Charlie Mazel

prominently: *in a noticeable way*

Quick Fact

J.B. Henry Savigny and Alexander Correard were two *Medusa* raft survivors. They said that they turned to cannibalism because their hunger and thirst had made them insane.

Artifacts help to date and identify the *Medusa* shipwreck. What else can you learn from the artifacts about the people and this period in history?

Take Note

The story of the *Medusa* is pretty incredible, but it is the horrific story of the raft that makes this shipwreck unforgettable. The raft was makeshift and overcrowded; there was no food or fresh water; people turned to cannibalism to stay alive; and many people died because rescue came too late. For these reasons, the *Medusa* is included on our list, with a #10 ranking.

• How do your feelings change when you learn that a disaster or accident was caused by human error?

5   4   3   2   1

Part of the **Breadalbane's** mast

TYPE OF SHIP: A British barque — a sailing ship with three masts, or poles, to support the sails

DATE OF SHIPWRECK: August 21, 1853

WHAT'S UNUSUAL: The *Breadalbane* (bred-awl-bayn) is the most northerly shipwreck ever discovered and the most well-preserved wreckage in the Arctic.

The barque *Breadalbane* was built in Scotland in 1843. It was a merchant ship that carried valuable goods all over the world.

The disaster of the *Breadalbane* started with the disappearance of a group of Arctic explorers in 1845. Sir John Franklin led an expedition to find the Northwest Passage — a navigational route linking the Atlantic and the Pacific Oceans. Many ships were sent to search for the explorers who went missing before they found the Northwest Passage. In the spring of 1853, the *Breadalbane* headed for the Arctic with supplies for a ship that was looking for Franklin and his crew.

Misfortune struck. The *Breadalbane* was trapped in an ice pack near Beechey Island, in present-day Nunavut, a territory in Northern Canada. The ice punctured the hull and the ship disappeared beneath the frigid waters. All 21 men onboard managed to survive.

Dr. Joseph MacInnis found the ship in August 1980, after searching for three years. Surprisingly, the wreck was preserved very well because of the extremely cold water of the Arctic. Let's read on to find out why the *Breadalbane* is #9 on our list.

Franklin and his crew died while looking for the Northwest Passage. What kind of personality does it take to be an explorer or adventurer?

BREADALBANE

WHERE IN THE WORLD?

The wreck was found in 338 feet of freezing Arctic water, about one mile south of Beechey Island. This island lies to the north of Resolute, a community in Nunavut (see map below). There was almost seven feet of surface ice above the water when the *Breadalbane* was found with its bow pointing eastward.

THAT SINKING FEELING ...

The *Breadalbane* had been trapped in ice for several days before it sank. Ice broke through the hull and it went down in only 15 minutes! All the men onboard jumped onto the ice and made their way to safety on their sister ship, the *Phoenix*.

---

bow: *forward part of the body of a ship*

? What were some challenges faced by expeditions to the Arctic in the 19th century? How are things different today?

WHAT'S DOWN THERE?

After years of hunting for the *Breadalbane*, Dr. Joseph MacInnis, a Canadian explorer, found success in 1980. The frosty, unpolluted waters of the Arctic had kept the ship in excellent condition. Explorers saw the bow, masts, rudder, and anchor. Lying upright on its keel, or spine, the *Breadalbane* was called the "perfect shipwreck" because it was so well preserved. The divers eventually brought up the big wooden wheel that was used to steer the ship.

IMPACT

The *Breadalbane* helped to expand our knowledge of the vast Canadian Arctic, deep-sea sailing, and cold-water diving. In 1980, MacInnis and his team had to use special underwater cameras to film the *Breadalbane*. Today, new technology allows scientists to dive deep into icy cold water to learn more about Arctic marine life. The *Breadalbane* is now a Canadian national monument, even though few people will ever get to see it!

---

rudder: *vertical blade at the back of a ship used to control direction*

Route of the Breadalbane

Devon Island · Greenland · Resolute · ✕ Beechey Island · Parry Channel · Baffin Bay · Disko Island · Prince of Wales Island · Baffin Island

The special diving suits invented to dive to the Breadalbane were called wasps.

The Expert Says...

"HMS *Breadalbane* is an opportunity for scientists to learn more about Arctic biology, geology, and sea ice. For historians, the wreck is a 'time capsule' containing nautical and personal objects from the mid-19th century."

— Dr. Joseph MacInnis, physician, scientist, and deep-sea explorer, who led the team that discovered the *Breadalbane*

INDEPTH: CLIMATE CHANGE

Online article from CBC News | March 24, 2005

Switch on the TV or radio these days, and you'll learn about icebergs melting and be bombarded with ads for movies depicting catastrophic weather disasters.

Melting iceberg

Climate change will not happen uniformly. … Scientists tend to point to the Arctic [North Pole] and the Antarctic [South Pole] climates as the signs of things to come. Climate change in those areas is expected to be close to three or four degrees in the winter months. That could lead to glacier melts, rising sea levels, and endangered Arctic wildlife.

catastrophic: *tragic; disastrous*
Arctic Climate Impact Assessment: *project that gathers and evaluates new information about climate change*
indigenous: *born in a region; native*

The Arctic Climate Impact Assessment from 2004 predicts a reduction in habitat for reindeer, musk ox, and caribou. Other studies have suggested polar bears could be threatened. Indigenous people will have their food and cultural systems disrupted. Thinning ice and rising sea levels will also threaten communities. …

In Canada, we can likely expect more heat-related deaths, more precipitation in certain locations, longer growing seasons, evaporating lakes, and rising sea levels. [The] Arctic region is likely to experience these things first, and people there have already begun to note the changes. …

Will polar bears become extinct as a result of climate change?

Global warming isn't affecting just the North and South Poles. How does it affect the rest of the world? If you don't know, find out. What can individuals do to stop global warming?

Quick Fact

The excellent condition of the wreck is helped by the absence of pollution and marine borers, a kind of mollusk or crustacean that eats sunken pieces of wood. They don't seem to like the cold!

Take Note

Attempts to find Franklin and the wreck of the *Breadalbane* helped map out previously uncharted territory and have given us important information about the Canadian Arctic. But the ship did not go down in a dramatic way and there was no loss of life. For these reasons, we rank the *Breadalbane* #9 on our list.
• Why is the mapping of uncharted territory important to navigation?

5   4   3   2   1

8 BISMARCK

A crowd of army and navy officials and Nazis gather to celebrate the launch of the Bismarck battleship in Hamburg, Germany.

BISMARCK LAUNCH—© BETTMANN/CORBIS

TYPE OF SHIP: The largest and most powerful German battleship of its time

DATE OF SHIPWRECK: May 27, 1941

WHAT'S UNUSUAL: It is the deepest shipwreck in this book, lying almost 15,420 feet below the surface of the water.

The *Bismarck* was one of the greatest battleships to sail the seas during World War II. It was named after Otto Fürst von Bismarck, the man who led the creation of the German Empire in the 1800s. In August of 1940, the *Bismarck* entered service in the German Navy. It was part of a new class of battleships that were built for strength and were much bigger than earlier ones.

Germany was at war with Britain. The Germans wanted to be in the North Atlantic to destroy British commercial and military ships. German forces also wanted to block shipments from the U.S. to Britain. Germany aimed to keep the British away from the Mediterranean because they had plans to invade that region.

On May 24, 1941, the Germans sank a prized British battleship called the HMS *Hood* and won the Battle of the Denmark Strait. These actions angered the British. They went after the *Bismarck*, which had become the target for revenge. The *Bismarck*'s naval career came to an end three days later, on May 27, 1941.

BISMARCK

WHERE IN THE WORLD?

The *Bismarck* rests in about 15,420 feet of water. Its hulk lies on the ocean floor over 400 miles west of Brest, France. It was found on the side of an underwater mountain that rises from a deep-ocean basin floor called the Porcupine Abyssal Plain.

THAT SINKING FEELING ...

After the Germans destroyed the HMS *Hood*, the British Navy seriously wanted to sink the *Bismarck*! They located the ship on May 26 and pounded it with torpedoes and gunfire. But the surviving sailors from the *Bismarck* claimed it wasn't this damage that brought the ship down. They claimed they were ordered to scuttle, or sink, the ship themselves, to avoid capture by the British.

? What would make you want to destroy something that is valuable to you?

WHAT'S DOWN THERE?

On June 8, 1989, four years after discovering the *Titanic*'s remains, Dr. Robert Ballard found the wreck of the *Bismarck*. It was more than 4,000 feet deeper than the *Titanic* wreck! Ballard used remote-controlled vehicles to dive to the wreck because it was so deep. The ship had been undisturbed until this time and the area was still littered with war machinery. Germany officially owns the wreck site and declares it a war grave. They do not allow anyone to explore the wreck.

? Is it more important to leave a site untouched and respect the dead or to explore the site and learn about history? Explain your answer.

IMPACT

The loss of the *Bismarck* had a great impact on World War II. Only 115 of the 2,200 sailors and officers onboard survived. With this shipwreck, Germany lost a great battleship and docked many of its other warships. It became much safer for the Allies transporting necessary supplies across the Atlantic Ocean. The sinking of the *Bismarck* might have helped the Allies to win the war.

Quick Fact
The *Bismarck* was originally built as a commerce raider. Its job was to attack its enemies' commercial ships.

The Expert Says ...
" We conclusively proved there was no way the British sank that ship. It was scuttled. "

— Dr. Alfred S. McLaren, naval expert who went down to the *Bismarck* in July and August 2002

BISMARCK

CHURCHILL TELLS DRAMATIC
STORY OF CHASE BY AIR AND SEA

— Excerpt from an article in the *Toronto Star*, May 27, 1941

London, May 27: British aerial torpedoes and shellfire sank the new 35,000-ton German battleship *Bismarck* in the Atlantic at 11 AM (5 AM E.D.T.) today.

The Royal Navy thus exacted vengeance for the *Bismarck's* sinking 72 hours ago of Britain's pride, the world's biggest warship, the 42,200-ton *Hood*.

His eyes gleaming with excitement, Prime Minister Winston Churchill personally announced the victory to parliament, and set the usually staid House of Commons wild with excitement. ...

First Venture into Open

One of the most powerful ships in the world [the *Bismarck*] had gone out from the Norwegian coast last Thursday on its first venture into the open sea. It scored one quick and dramatic triumph. Five days later it went down in battle. From the day that it left Norway, it was disclosed today, the British fleet had stalked it.

Over thousands of miles of sea, from the Greenland-Iceland area to the French invasion coast, British battleships and other units closed in. Night and day scout planes sought it. When they sighted it and flashed its position, torpedo planes dived down on it.

Seeking to rid itself of its pursuers during the few northern hours of darkness or in the fogs, which form suddenly over the Arctic and sub-Arctic seas, it had sought to reach the European coast, and safety, and failed.

E.D.T.: *Eastern Daylight Time*
staid: *serious; calm*
stalked: *followed secretly*

HMS HOOD

Quick Fact

A total of 2,876 shells were fired at the *Bismarck*, but only four were able to get through its hull.

Take Note

We remember the shipwreck of the *Bismarck* for the major loss of lives and the role it played in the German Navy during World War II. The challenge in finding this lost ship adds to the impact — it required deep-sea searching, sophisticated technology, and some good luck.
• What makes this shipwreck more unforgettable than the *Breadalbane*? Make a list with your reasons.

? Note the headline and the mood expressed in this news article about the sinking of the *Bismarck*. What does this tell you about the politics of the time?

(7) THE ULUBURUN

*Archeologists examining
the Uluburun wreck on
the ocean floor*

WRECK DIVERS–COURTESY OF THE INSTITUTE OF NAUTICAL ARCHAEOLOGY; BACKGROUND–SHUTTERSTOCK

SHIPWRECK

TYPE OF SHIP: A 50-foot-long merchant ship

DATE OF SHIPWRECK: Around the 14th century B.C.

WHAT'S UNUSUAL: Named after Uluburun (oo-loo-boo-roon) Bay because no one knows the original name of this ship. The Uluburun shipwreck is the oldest known shipwreck in the world.

In 1982, Mehmet Cakir was diving for sponge in the Mediterranean Sea off the coast of Turkey, but he ended up discovering something much more valuable. He found a large pile of copper ingots that led him to the wreck of an ancient vessel! Scientists and explorers started to bring up the fascinating and educational treasures of a 3,300-year-old merchant vessel. The full excavation of the site took 10 years with divers bringing up over 18,000 artifacts!

The artifacts date back to the Bronze Age, a time when people used bronze weapons and artifacts before they switched to iron. The artifacts and items from the wreck came from six civilizations — they were Canaan, Mycenaean, Cypriot, Kassite, Egyptian, and Assyrian in origin. These items have given us valuable information about ancient shipping and trading routes and this period in ancient history. Nobody knows how or why the ship sank, but we'll never forget this historic shipwreck and its treasures. That's why it is #7 on our list of most unforgettable shipwrecks.

ingots: *oblong bars of metal*
excavation: *digging a large hole*

THE ULUBURUN SHIPWRECK

WHERE IN THE WORLD?

The ship was found off the coast of Turkey in Uluburun Bay, near the city of Kas. It lies on a steep slope on the ocean floor. The stern is 170 feet down and the bow 145 feet deep. The cargo was found even further down the slope at a depth of 197 feet.

THAT SINKING FEELING ...

Nobody knows for sure how or why the ship sank. It might have been pushed by the wind into the rocky shore. The hull, or body, of the ship was broken. This might have caused the sinking.

WHAT'S DOWN THERE?

Thousands of artifacts were recovered from the wreck. Divers also found enough copper and tin to make 11 tons of bronze! They also found gold and large pieces of expensive ivory. It is possible that the items onboard were gifts for a king or pharaoh.

? Divers found weapons, copper, jewelry, tools, and other items at the site of the wreck. What might we learn from studying these historic items?

IMPACT

A lot of what was learned from the Uluburun shipwreck has to do with shipbuilding and trade. The ship provides the earliest known example of mortise-and-tenon joinery. The number of items from Canaan (now part of Israel) challenged the old belief that the Canaanites were not strong traders. The artifacts have given us an idea of what life was like at that time in history.

---

stern: *back, or rear, of a ship*
mortise-and-tenon joinery: *strongest and most common type of joint in woodworking*

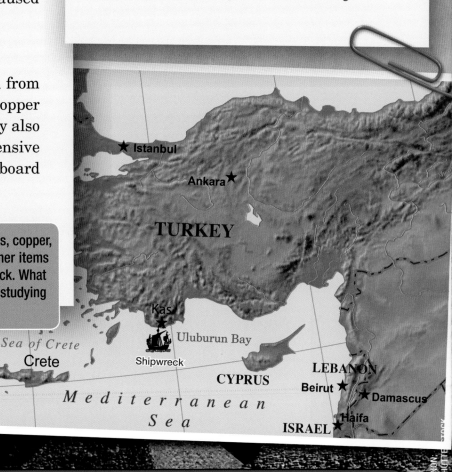

TURKEY
★ Istanbul
Ankara ★
Kas
Uluburun Bay
Sea of Crete
Crete
Shipwreck
CYPRUS
LEBANON
Beirut ★
★ Damascus
Mediterranean Sea
Haifa
ISRAEL ★

Quick Fact
Copper and tin are mixed together to make bronze. Bronze does not rust easily. It is a harder material than copper.

The Expert Says...

"It has been called by some archeologists outside our group the most important Late Bronze Age site excavated in the second half of the 20th century."

— George Bass, leader of the first archeological underwater visit to the Uluburun site

IT'S ANYBODY'S GUESS!

The Uluburun shipwreck is a mystery that scientists and marine archeologists have been trying to piece together since the discovery of the lost ship in 1982. No one knows where it was going, where it came from, or why it sank. But, as you can see in this article, there are some pretty good guesses!

The ship was at sea at about the time when King Tutankhamen ruled Egypt, and when Troy, Greece, was a successful city. Scientists think the ship might have left the coast of Syria and stopped at Cyprus for the copper ingots it was carrying. All the weapons onboard, including swords, bows and arrows, and spears, suggest that the ship's crew was worried about being attacked, or that they were transporting weapons to a battle. It's likely that strong winds and underwater currents pushed the vessel too close to the shore causing it to sink after hitting the rocks.

It's hard to look fresh after 3,300 years! The ship's age might be creeping up on it, but at least scientists say that pollution hasn't done much, if any, damage to the ship. This is because the wreck lies in a fairly remote area off the coast of Turkey. The main hazards at the site are sharks and the scorpion fish that live on the seafloor and have spines that contain venom!

King Tutankhamen's golden death mask

What clues would you look for to determine how a ship went down? Make a list.

The ship may have picked up copper ingots from Cyprus.

Quick Fact

Because of the ship's depth, the divers could only go down to the wreck for 20 minutes at a time, twice a day. There were a total of 22,413 dives, totaling 6,613 hours.

Take Note

You are not likely to hear about the Uluburun shipwreck because it happened so long ago and there are no records about it. We do not know who owned it, how it sank, or how many lives were lost. But, its discovery has given us new knowledge about six ancient civilizations in history. It is a great archeological discovery and this is why we rank it higher than the other shipwrecks we have read about so far.
• Would you rank the Uluburun shipwreck higher than the *Bismarck*? Why?

5   4   3   2   1

(6) L'ORIENT

This painting shows the explosion of L'Orient. *It is titled* The Battle of the Nile *and was painted by Philip James de Loutherbourg (1740–1812).*

TYPE OF SHIP: An enormous battleship with 124 cannons — the flagship of Napoleon's navy

DATE OF SHIPWRECK: August 1, 1798

WHAT'S UNUSUAL: *L'Orient* (loh-ree-ahn) exploded and sank in battle — ending Napoleon's dream of controlling Egypt and the East.

Napoleon Bonaparte was a man with big ideas — an ambitious leader of France and Italy in the late 18th and early 19th centuries. He wanted to take over as much of Europe as possible.

In 1798, Napoleon sailed to the Mediterranean hoping to conquer Egypt. This would protect the trade route France had set up and limit Britain's access to India. Unfortunately, the British wanted to stop him. Admiral Nelson of the British Navy saw his chance in the Bay of Aboukir (ah-boo-keer), where the French had anchored their fleet of 13 ships. This was a good location for a battle — the British knew there was no escape once they blocked the entrance to the sea. They launched a surprise attack!

Napoleon suffered heavy losses in the battle. By the time it ended, only two French ships were left afloat and a large number of French military men were killed. The biggest blow was the sinking of *L'Orient*, which exploded in a gigantic ball of fire. With such heavy losses, Napoleon was defeated and the British Navy took control of the seas.

---

flagship: *main vessel of a shipping line*

L'ORIENT

WHERE IN THE WORLD?

L'Orient was anchored in the Bay of Aboukir, about 16 miles northeast of Alexandria, Egypt, on the Nile Delta. The ship exploded with so much force that the fireball could be seen 12 miles away. The battle stopped for a short time while people watched *L'Orient* go down in flames.

THAT SINKING FEELING ...

British Admiral Nelson surrounded Napoleon's fleet by surprise at around six o'clock in the evening. *L'Orient* was carrying so much gunpowder that it didn't take long to explode in a massive ball of fire. When the wreck was discovered in 1983, only pieces of the hull were left. Franck Goddio, the marine archeologist in the search, found pieces of the ship scattered over 125 acres of seabed.

WHAT'S DOWN THERE?

Only the midsection of *L'Orient* was found, suggesting that both the bow and the stern were destroyed. Explorers uncovered a treasure trove of gold, silver, and copper coins. They also found Napoleon's printing press, cannons, weapons, and medical equipment for surgery in the wreckage — and even skeletal remains.

IMPACT

About 1,000 men, including the leader of the French Navy, died on *L'Orient*. Napoleon lost much of his personal wealth and all the valuables carried on this flagship. The loss of *L'Orient* changed the course of history — Napoleon abandoned his dreams of controlling Egypt and the Middle East. The British became the dominant power on the high seas.

? Why was naval power so important in the 18th century?

A cannon from Napoleon's fleet

? Think like a marine archeologist. What might be other challenges to uncovering a wreck that is so spread out?

Quick Fact

Divers at the wreck site claim that they can still smell gunpowder from the battle! Do you think this is possible?

The Expert Says...

" Everything was scattered around *L'Orient*. To give you an idea of the blast, the distance between the two more distant cannons is about 770 feet. "

— Franck Goddio, marine archeologist and explorer of *L'Orient*

Battle of the Nile

Here is a comparison chart of the battle that took place on the Bay of Aboukir. On one side were the British, led by Navy Commander Admiral Nelson. On the other were the French, led by Admiral Brueys, Navy Commander, and Napoleon Bonaparte, the military leader in charge of the mission.

? Napoleon anchored his fleet in the Bay of Aboukir because of a change of plan. So was it luck or military strategy that led to the British victory? Explain your answer.

The British		The French
Had 14 vessels with guns and ammunition, but fewer weapons than the French.	**Guns and Ships**	Had 13 vessels with more powerful guns than the British.
Surrounded the French fleet and attacked from both sides by surprise. They fought as a team and with a plan.	**Strategy**	Were taken by surprise. They had more ammunition and men, but did not expect to be surrounded or attacked.
Lost only two vessels. Victory strengthened the war against France and secured Britain's access to the East and India.	**Outcome**	The losses destroyed Napoleon's plan to conquer Egypt and the Middle East. The French suffered a major defeat in trying to take over Europe.
Admiral Nelson became an international hero.	**Fate of Leaders**	Eventually, Napoleon was defeated at another battle called Waterloo. He died powerless and in exile.
No known record.	**Wreckage**	Marine archeologist Franck Goddio concluded that two major explosions in the front and back of the ship caused the extensive damage to *L'Orient*.

exile: *forced removal from home country*

Quick Fact

Orient is another word for East Asia. *L'Orient* refers to Napoleon's dream to take over Asia and India.

Admiral Nelson's ship, the HMS *Victory*

Take Note

L'Orient certainly went down with a bang! Almost 1,000 men were killed, and Napoleon lost his personal wealth, morale, and ambition. *L'Orient* had a direct impact on Napoleon but the ship's sinking doesn't really affect us today. For these reasons, we place *L'Orient* #6 on our list.

• Compare *L'Orient* to the *Bismarck* at #8. Using two columns, list the similarities and differences. Would you switch their ranking? What factors would you consider?

5   4   3   2   1

Britannic was the largest passenger ship of its time. It was torpedoed in the Aegean while doing duty as a hospital ship.

HMHS BRITANNIC—©BETTMANN/CORBIS

TYPE OF SHIP: A passenger ocean liner that was converted into a hospital ship

DATE OF SHIPWRECK: November 21, 1916

WHAT'S UNUSUAL: The HMHS (His/Her Majesty's Hospital Ship) *Britannic* was a sister ship to the *Titanic* and was rebuilt with added safety features to make it "unsinkable."

The White Star Line was a shipping company that was doing booming business in the late 1800s and early 1900s. The company built three luxurious ocean passenger liners: the *Titanic*, *Britannic*, and *Olympic*. The *Britannic* and the *Olympic* were both overhauled and partially redesigned to make them safer after the sinking of the *Titanic*.

The *Britannic* was built as a passenger ship. However, when World War I broke out, it was turned into a hospital ship and sent into service. In November 1916, it set sail for the Mediterranean to pick up wounded soldiers. But, just after 8:00 AM on the morning of November 21, a loud explosion was heard onboard the ship. Whether it was a torpedo or a mine, something tore a huge hole in the starboard, or right-hand, side of the ship. It didn't take long before the *Britannic* was lying on the ocean floor.

HMHS BRITANNIC

WHERE IN THE WORLD?

The *Britannic* lies about 400 feet underwater, off the Island of Kea, southeast of Athens, Greece. Oddly, its current location is not where the British Navy claims that it sank. Some believe the confusion about the location was a cover-up to prevent explorers from finding clues that might point to the British Navy's guilt. Even though it was a hospital ship, the Germans claimed that the *Britannic* was carrying military weapons!

> **?** What other reasons can you think of to explain why the *Britannic's* final resting place is different from where it was supposed to have sunk?

THAT SINKING FEELING . . .

No one has been able to prove whether the *Britannic* hit a mine or if a torpedo struck it. The German U-boat in the area had no record of torpedoing a ship. After the explosion, water flooded through the open portholes and into the ship. The *Britannic* sank in just about 55 minutes.

U-boat: *submarine*

Quick Fact

There are many theories about the sinking of the *Britannic*. Some people think the coal storage area exploded. Others think the ship may have been sunk by its own crew to gain the sympathy of the Americans.

The Expert Says...

" [Passengers] thought they saw what they took to be a torpedo miss the rudder, and a second one find us in the bow. **"**

— Rev. John Fleming, author of *The Last Voyage of HMHS Britannic*

WHAT'S DOWN THERE?

Famous underwater explorer Jacques Cousteau found the wreck in 1975. The huge ship lies almost intact on the seafloor. There were few treasures, as it was a hospital ship. The wreck has been declared a war grave, so divers need permission from the British and Greek governments to visit the site.

> **?** The *Britannic* was a British ship but sank in Greek territory in the Aegean Sea. Who do you think should own the wreck? Does one country have more right to the wreck than the other? Why?

IMPACT

The sinking of a hospital ship, considered off-limits to the enemy, angered British citizens and increased their support of World War I against Germany. The ship was flying a red cross to show that it was a hospital ship and not armed. The sinking of the *Britannic* was one of the reasons that the U.S. was motivated to join the war. Of the 1,134 passengers and medical crew onboard, 41 were injured and 30 died as they tried to get away on lifeboats.

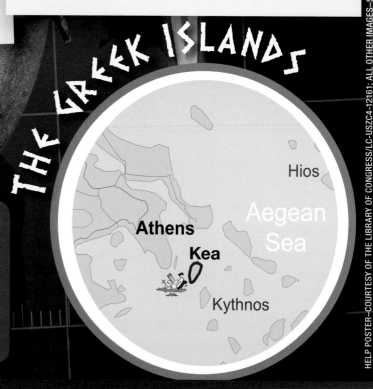

THE GREEK ISLANDS

Hios

Athens

Aegean Sea

Kea

Kythnos

8 7 6

Underwater Explorer

Below is an excerpt of an interview with Dr. Robert Ballard, President of the Institute for Exploration, Connecticut. Dr. Ballard visited the wreck site in 1995.

Q: What are the pros and cons of our newfound ability to find these magnificent shipwrecks?

BALLARD: ... Up until recently, all underwater archeological discoveries have been done in a water depth of less than 200 feet. Well, 200 feet is less than four percent of the world's oceans. But this new technology of submersibles and robots can now cover 97 percent of the world's oceans. ... There's probably more history now preserved underwater than in all the museums of the world combined. And there's no law governing that history. It's finders' keepers. Who's the finder, a good guy or a bad guy?

Q: Isn't there an argument to be made for ... taking artifacts from [a] ship, and putting them in a museum where people can see them and learn from them?

BALLARD: [People are] bringing up artifacts for commercial gain. These people are not historians, they're not archeologists ... [There] are ships of antiquity and ships of historical importance that are not protected from unscrupulous people.

Q: Can you describe your vision for an undersea museum in more detail?

BALLARD: Basically, we want to place cameras on the *Britannic* that are then controlled from our new exhibit center in Mystic, Connecticut — but, ultimately, can be controlled by anyone on the information highway. It's not a great deal of technology to place permanent visitation technology on the *Britannic* and have people access it ...

---

unscrupulous: *lacking principles; not acting according to right and wrong*
information highway: *cyberspace; online world*

Quick Fact

Violet Jessop was a nurse and steward who worked on all three doomed White Star ships. Why do you think Violet would work on the *Britannic* after surviving the disaster of the *Titanic*?

Take Note

The HMHS *Britannic* is one of many ships in this book that went down during wartime. It is not surprising to lose ships in a war, but the *Britannic* was a hospital ship and was supposed to be the world's most "unsinkable" ship. The *Britannic*'s sinking raised concerns regarding shipbuilding, design, maintenance, and safety for passengers and crew.
• How should the fact that so few lives were lost affect the *Britannic*'s ranking?

5

3

2

1

The steam liner Empress of Ireland shortly before the collision with a freighter that caused it to sink off the coast of Quebec, Canada

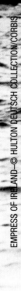

IRELAND

TYPE OF SHIP: A Canadian Pacific ocean liner with a capacity of 1,580 passengers

DATE OF SHIPWRECK: May 29, 1914

WHAT'S UNUSUAL: This is the worst maritime disaster in Canadian history — a collision with another ship killed 1,012 passengers onboard the *Empress of Ireland*.

The *Empress of Ireland* was the pride of the Canadian Pacific Railway company. This flagship vessel was said to be one of the largest, fastest, and most reliable ships to travel the North Atlantic. Its job was to bring passengers from Liverpool, England, to Quebec City, where they could then board a train to Western Canada.

For eight years, the *Empress of Ireland* offered safety and luxury for passengers. On the fateful night of May 29, 1914, a thick fog rolled onto the St. Lawrence River, making everything look unfamiliar. By the time the captains of the *Empress* and the Norwegian ship the *Storstad* realized they were headed straight for each other, it was too late. Within 14 minutes, the *Empress of Ireland* sank. Even though the ship had more than enough lifeboats, about 75 percent of those onboard died. This is still the worst maritime disaster in Canadian history. The place where the *Empress* sank is now a protected site. Sadly, this tragedy was soon forgotten because World War I began shortly after the ship sank.

EMPRESS OF IRELAND

WHERE IN THE WORLD?

The ship went down near Rimouski in Quebec, Canada, in the St. Lawrence River. The water there is very cold and the current is strong and dangerous. The wreck of the *Empress* lies about 150 feet deep. Only very experienced scuba divers can go down to the wreck.

Quick Fact

The St. Lawrence River runs almost 745 miles from the Thousand Islands in Ontario, Canada, to the Gaspé Peninsula in Quebec. It is not easy to navigate because of rapids, marshes, ice formations, and thick fog.

THAT SINKING FEELING ...

It was extremely foggy when the Norwegian *Storstad* rammed into the *Empress of Ireland*. The *Empress* was barely 12 hours into its journey to Liverpool and it was the middle of the night. Two of the ship's watertight compartments were damaged and water got in through portholes that had been left open. When the ship tipped over, it quickly flooded. The death toll was huge — 1,012 of the 1,477 onboard died. The *Storstad* did not sink.

WHAT'S DOWN THERE?

After the *Empress* sank, Canadian Pacific hired people to salvage some of the items from the wreck. The team brought up silver bars and mail that was going to England. The sediment and strong current at the bottom of the river cover and uncover the ship's treasures frequently, so divers discover something different each time they dive.

IMPACT

The *Storstad* punctured the *Empress* all the way down the side, allowing water to get in and sink it. After the tragedy, bows were redesigned to keep the puncture above the waterline if a ship is hit. New rules required all portholes and watertight doors to be closed at night and in foggy weather. Lifeboats had to be positioned so that they could be easily released if a ship tipped on its side. Rules were also put in place so ships did not pass too close to one another.

sediment: *matter (silt, sand, and gravel) that settles at the bottom of a liquid*

 This tragedy didn't get as much attention as it might have because of the start of World War I. Why might news of the war have overshadowed news of the shipwreck?

Advection fog is created when warm air moves over a cool mass of water. This is probably what happened over the St. Lawrence the night of this tragedy.

The Expert Says...

"Even though the *Empress of Ireland* carried more than enough lifeboats and radio equipment, the rate of flooding at over 60,000 gallons per second made these items of little use to the sleepy passengers left struggling for survival in a dark ship sinking quickly.

— Heather Knowles and David Caldwell, diving experts and authors of *The Empress of Ireland: An Essay*

YOU BE THE JUDGE

An inquiry was held after the sinking of the *Empress of Ireland* to determine who was at fault. Read both sides of the story in the table below.

Case No. 4	*Empress of Ireland v. Storstad*
Plaintiff: *Empress of Ireland*	**Defendant: *Storstad***
The portholes were open, which was against the rules.	The *Storstad* had a very sharp bow to break away icebergs.
Captain Henry George Kendall was on his first voyage.	First Mate Alfred Toftenes, the second in command after the captain, believed the ships would pass port to port, the way ships usually passed each other.
When Kendall saw the *Storstad*, he signaled that he would pass starboard-to-starboard, or right side to right side.	The Norwegians blamed Captain Kendall for the sinking because he passed starboard instead of port, which is more common.
The ship carried 2,212 life jackets and had enough lifeboats for all passengers.	The Norwegians tried to keep ramming into the *Empress* after they hit to make a seal and keep the water out, but the current made them drift apart.
Only one SOS call was sent out before flooding cut off the ship's power.	At the time of the accident, the captain was in bed. He had left the first mate in charge. The first mate was supposed to call the captain if fog rolled in.
The watertight doors sometimes had to be opened to allow passengers to get around, but some were not closed again.	port: *left-hand side*

EXHIBIT B

CONFIDENTIAL

Quick Fact

Divers found almost 600 bodies on the wreck. Only four children survived. One of them, Grace Hannagan Martyn, died at 88 years old in 1988.

RIMOUSKI - VICTIMS "EMP. OF IRELAND"

EXHIBIT A

Take Note

The *Empress of Ireland* is one of two ships in this book that sank in a river. With a death toll of 1,012, it is unforgettable as the worst maritime disaster in Canadian history. After the wreck, shipping regulations were enforced, making traveling by ship much safer for everyone.
• Fog was the cause of this shipwreck. What other weather conditions could be dangerous to a ship at sea? Make a list.

5 **4** 3 2 1

3 TITANIC

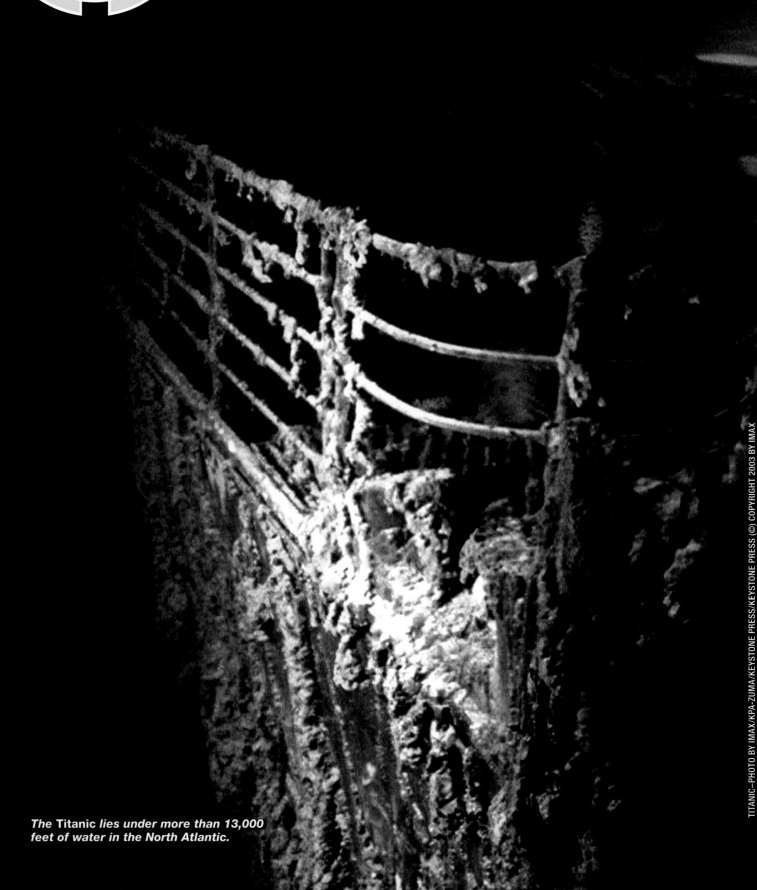

The Titanic lies under more than 13,000 feet of water in the North Atlantic.

TYPE OF SHIP: A deluxe, "unsinkable" passenger liner

DATE OF SHIPWRECK: April 15, 1912

WHAT'S UNUSUAL: The *Titanic* hit an iceberg only five days into its first voyage across the Atlantic.

On that fateful morning, the world woke up to stunning news. The *Titanic*, the "unsinkable" ship built for speed, strength, and safety, had gone down in the icy waters of the North Atlantic. It had hit an iceberg!

Onboard were some of America's wealthiest and most famous people of the time — among them were John Jacob Astor, Benjamin Guggenheim, and Isidor and Ida Straus. The *Titanic* was publicized as the most modern ship of its time, complete with a swimming pool, gymnasium, library, and squash court. It was the *Titanic*'s first voyage, and people were eager to be a part of history.

It took less than three hours for the ship to fill with water, break in two parts, and sink deep into the ocean. Approximately 1,500 people died, and the story of the *Titanic* continues to capture the imagination of generations. This famed ship has become the subject of songs, books, a Broadway musical, and award-winning movies.

TITANIC

WHERE IN THE WORLD?

When it hit the iceberg, the *Titanic* was approximately 400 miles south of Newfoundland, a province in Eastern Canada. The wreck was found beneath almost 13,000 feet of water and had moved quite a distance from where it originally sank. It was found 450 miles southeast of Newfoundland.

? Why do you think the shipwreck was not found exactly where it was reported to have sunk? Suggest all possible reasons.

THAT SINKING FEELING ...

Before it sank, several messages were sent to the *Titanic* from other ocean liners warning of icebergs that had been brought down by the Labrador Current. The captain received some of the warnings but wasn't too worried — ice in the Atlantic was common in April. At 11:40 that evening, the man on lookout saw icebergs straight ahead and sounded the alarm. Sadly, the *Titanic* didn't have enough lifeboats for all of the crew and passengers. The *Titanic* sent a distress call to the *Californian*, the closest ship at the time of the accident. But, the radio operator of the *Californian* had turned the radio off and gone to bed. He never received the distress call.

WHAT'S DOWN THERE?

Dr. Robert Ballard found the stern section of the *Titanic* about 2,000 feet away from the bow of the ship. A variety of artifacts have been recovered, including the ship's bells and a 17-ton section of the hull. Porcelain dishes from the first-class dining room, jewelry, brushes, and even bottles of perfume have also been recovered.

IMPACT

The sinking of the *Titanic* resulted in the creation of an international convention called SOLAS (Safety of Life at Sea). Their purpose was to set up safety guidelines for passenger vessels. The guidelines stated that ships needed enough lifeboats for all passengers, that safety drills must be practiced, that radio communication would operate continuously, and that red rockets fired from ships meant they were in distress. Another important change was made to hull construction. Ships were later designed with double hulls for strength.

Quick Fact

The *Titanic* was the largest ship of its time, measuring almost 890 feet long, 90 feet wide, and 175 feet high. That makes the *Titanic* about four city blocks long and 11 stories high.

The Titanic prepares to be launched.

The Expert Says...

" Finding the ship was difficult because of the North Atlantic's unpredictable weather, the enormous depth at which *Titanic* lies, and conflicting accounts of her final moments. "

— Dr. Robert Ballard, oceanographer who discovered the wreck of the *Titanic* in 1985

INSIDE ICEBERGS

They may be broken-off bits of glaciers, but don't underestimate the power of icebergs! Ninety percent of their size is hidden below the surface of the water, so these massive pieces of floating ice can mean serious danger to ocean travelers. Read this article to find out more about these hazards of the high seas.

Glaciers are formed when the buildup of thousands of years of snowfall turns into ice. Icebergs are simply pieces that are calved by the glacier, and begin to drift in the ocean. After they are calved, icebergs drift for two to three years along the Baffin Current and then the Labrador Current until they get to the coast of Newfoundland. Only about one percent of icebergs ever make it to the Atlantic Ocean, but this is still enough to have an impact!

calved: *broken off*

Off the coast of Newfoundland, icebergs enter the infamous "Iceberg Alley." Here a huge number of icebergs enter shipping lanes and make navigation a difficult task! This dangerous area, located about 250 miles southeast of Newfoundland, was where the *Titanic*, and hundreds of others, met a terrible fate.

Quick Fact

Icebergs are normally white because of all the tiny air bubbles. The bubbles reflect all light waves, giving the iceberg a white appearance.

The *Titanic* sets off on its fateful journey.

Take Note

The *Titanic* is one of the most famous shipwrecks of all time and has been immortalized in books, songs, and movies. It had a high death toll and sank in a dramatic way. It hit an iceberg and split in half as it sank. Its sinking has had a positive impact on passenger safety at sea and shipping rules and standards for ocean vessels. The deep-water location of the wreck has increased our understanding of deep-sea geography and ocean conditions. The *Titanic* will never be forgotten and we rank it #3 on our list.
• What is it about the *Titanic* tragedy that has captured people's attention for so long?

5　　**3**　　**2**　　**1**

2 SULTANA

The Sultana before an explosion sank it in the Mississippi River

TYPE OF SHIP: An American steamboat

DATE OF SHIPWRECK: April 27, 1865

WHAT'S UNUSUAL: The *Sultana* exploded and sank on the Mississippi River, killing more than 1,600 people.

In April of 1865, the American Civil War was drawing to a close. Union soldiers who had fought in the South were released from war camps and going home. Private boats, among them the *Sultana*, were hired to transport these soldiers, at a cost of $5 per soldier and $10 per officer. Money-hungry officials packed the boat to over six times its passenger capacity and legal limit.

On April 27, 1865, an explosion ripped through the *Sultana,* killing more than 1,600 passengers on the crowded ship. It was the worst maritime disaster in U.S. history!

So what caused the explosion? Some said that the boilers exploded because they had been poorly repaired. Others believed a torpedo sank the boat. Still others thought a bomb was planted by a Southerner who was angry that the South had lost the war.

This disastrous tragedy did not receive the attention it deserved because people were too distracted with news about the Civil War. However, it is an unforgettable event in U.S. history and ranks #2 on our list.

SULTANA

WHERE IN THE WORLD?

The *Sultana* was about seven miles north of Memphis, Tennessee, when there was an explosion. Once this happened, the ship could not continue its journey north on the Mississippi River. It eventually went down near Memphis. Passengers who survived the initial blast were thrown into the water, which was deeper and rougher than usual because of the time of year.

THAT SINKING FEELING ...

There was evidence that one of the ship's boilers was damaged before the journey. It had received a quick patch job so that it could set sail without any delay. In the middle of the night, an explosion blew the ship apart and set it on fire. Those who survived had to face fire, falling debris, and the cold, rough waters of the Mississippi.

Soldier from the American Civil War

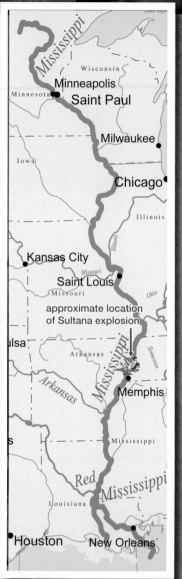

approximate location of Sultana explosion

WHAT'S DOWN THERE?

Sadly, there was little left of the *Sultana* after the explosion and fires. Today, the wreckage is buried 20 feet below a field in Arkansas, about two miles from the current position of the Mississippi River. The wreckage of the *Sultana* now lies under soil and not water. This is because the Mississippi River has carved a new path. The river has changed its course over time because of erosion.

IMPACT

Almost 1,700 people died on the *Sultana*. Many of these were soldiers who had survived the war and were finally going home. An investigation into the explosion didn't confirm what had caused it. But many believed that overcrowding and damaged boilers were to blame and that this accident was preventable. After the accident, safety regulations were enforced.

 If you were reading the newspaper in 1865, would you want to read about the *Sultana* or about the Civil War? Explain your answer.

The Expert Says...

" [The *Sultana*] was the worst maritime disaster in U.S. history, more costly than even the April 14, 1912, sinking of the *Titanic* ... "

— Stephen Ambrose, American historian and professor at the University of New Orleans

Quick Fact

The *Sultana* had a lot of safety equipment for its time — safety gauges on the boilers, firefighting equipment, lifeboats, and life preservers.

STORY OF A SURVIVOR

This personal account describes what happened on the day of the tragedy.

I was awakened by the noise of a terrific explosion of the boilers, and found myself being hurled upward through the air. I must have gone up about 20 or 25 feet. In falling I struck the shattered pilothouse. My face was cut and bleeding, and my hair was half singed off by a flame that burst over me. ...

The night was moonless, but the flames spread a bright gleam over the swollen stream. Never can I forget that scene. ... Every few minutes a hand would be uplifted helplessly, and the next moment its owner would be swept out of my sight.

The flames grew hotter, and approached more nearly. My place of observation could be held but a little longer. To remain would be to burn to death. To jump would be to drown, for I was an indifferent swimmer. The increasing heat decided me. I sprang into the water. ... At last, when my strength was almost exhausted, I was struck from behind, and turning about, grasped a floating piece of timber that had probably been a deck support. I threw my arms over it, and in an hour had floated into the branches of a tree that overhung the swollen river. I clambered to a place of safety. Four others found places in the tree. Here we remained until daylight, when one of the many boats that had been sent up from Memphis for the relief of the survivors approached near enough to hear our cries. ...

Mr. Schirmeyer
— survivor of the *Sultana*

pilothouse: *structure on ship containing steering wheel and compass*

indifferent: *neither good nor bad*

Quick Fact

The *Sultana* was built to carry about 375 passengers. On the day it sank, it was overloaded with more than 2,000 people! The ship was so overcrowded that the decks had additional supports added to prevent sagging.

Take Note

The circumstances surrounding the sinking of the *Sultana* place it at #2 on our list. To this day, there is no conclusive evidence to determine if it exploded because of an accident or sabotage, even though many thought the ship's boilers caused the explosion. Like the *Medusa* at #10, the *Sultana* is buried under soil. But unlike the *Medusa*, its death toll is so high that it is considered the worst maritime disaster in U.S. history.

• Is a shipwreck that is buried under soil more or less interesting than one that lies at the bottom of the ocean? Give reasons to support your answer.

5   4   3   2

1 USS ARIZONA

The USS Arizona exploded after it was hit by a Japanese bomb, December 7, 1941.

PEARL HARBOR—THE GRANGER COLLECTION, NEW YORK; ZERO—ISTOCK; ALL OTHER IMAGES—SHUTTERSTOCK

The morning of December 7, 1941, was sunny, peaceful, and beautiful at Pearl Harbor, located on the Hawaiian Island of Oahu. Pearl Harbor was home to U.S. Navy ships and personnel. Just after 8:00 AM though, this calm harbor was changed forever. Japanese planes suddenly filled the skies and bombs started to drop on the Navy ships.

On the morning of the attack, the USS *Arizona* was anchored on the southeast corner of Ford Island, within Pearl Harbor. It had been at the Hawaiian naval base for months, with its crew completing "battle-readiness" drills. A bomb weighing more than 1,765 pounds hit the USS *Arizona* and sank it within nine minutes. The ship was totally destroyed in the attack.

The *Arizona* was never moved from the location where it sank. A memorial now stands directly over the hull and visitors can see part of the ship's remains. The memorial consists of a white covered bridge that holds a museum. There is also a room that has the names of the men who died on the *Arizona* and another ship, the USS *Utah*. Read on to find out why the USS *Arizona* is the most unforgettable shipwreck on our list.

USS ARIZONA

Japanese Zero fighter planes led the attack on Pearl Harbor.

WHERE IN THE WORLD?

Pearl Harbor is a natural, clover-shaped harbor on the island of Oahu. It is about six miles west of Honolulu, the capital city of Hawaii. Ford Island lies within the harbor. The USS *Arizona* was stationed in "Battleship Row," with six other battleships, on the southeast side of Ford Island when it was attacked.

THAT SINKING FEELING ...

The USS *Arizona* took two direct hits and three near misses on December 7, 1941. The bomb that hit it ignited its store of ammunition. The ship exploded, broke in half, and sank within nine minutes.

WHAT'S DOWN THERE?

The damage to the USS *Arizona* was so great that it could not be saved after it sank. A few guns were removed but the rest of the ship lies below 40 feet of water, exactly where it went down. The ship leaks about two quarts of oil a day, and these oil droplets are called "black tears." The USS *Arizona* is considered a graveyard since the remains of many who died onboard are still there. Many sailors who survived the attack on the USS *Arizona* have their ashes buried with their comrades after they die.

IMPACT

There was destruction and death everywhere. The ship was carrying almost 500 tons of gunpowder and burned for two days. In total, 1,177 out of about 1,470 men onboard died during the attack. On the day after the Pearl Harbor attack, the United States declared war on Japan and joined the Allies in the war. The Allies, including the United Kingdom and the Soviet Union, grew in strength and defeated the Axis nations, led by Japan and Germany.

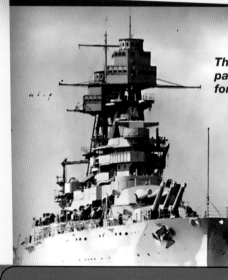

The USS *Arizona* patrols the Pacific for enemy ships.

? Why do you think survivors would want their ashes buried there?

Quick Fact

The USS *Arizona* was 6,000 feet long, or three times the size of the Statue of Liberty in New York City.

Some of the wreck of the USS Arizona *is actually visible above water.*

The Expert Says...

" Pearl Harbor and the ensuing war was a crucial turning point for various nations, including the United States. "

— Dr. Craig Symonds, professor, U.S. Naval Academy

REMEMBERING PEARL HARBOR

The bombing of Pearl Harbor is an important day in the history of the United States. It was a horrific and unforgettable event, as shown by the numbers in the list below.

Today, tourists can visit the memorial site for the USS *Arizona*; it stands directly above the exact spot where the ship went under. Every year, millions pay their respects to the sailors who lost their lives. The sailors' names are engraved on the wall of the memorial, which also holds the original bells that were salvaged from the battleship. Seven windows mark the date of the attack. Through the floor of the memorial you can see what remains of the battleship.

The USS Arizona Memorial at Pearl Harbor

1,500,000 ▷ approximate number of annual visitors to the USS *Arizona* memorial

1,400,000 ▷ gallons of fuel on the *Arizona* when it sank

$500,000 ▷ cost to build the memorial

400,000 ▷ approximate number of U.S. casualties in World War II

2,390 ▷ total number of Americans killed during the attack

353 ▷ number of Japanese aircraft in the attack

323 ▷ number of U.S. aircraft destroyed or damaged in the attack

103 ▷ number of Japanese aircraft destroyed or damaged

21 ▷ number of U.S. sailing vessels sunk or damaged

5 ▷ number of Japanese ships sunk or damaged

$0 ▷ cost to take the tour and visit the USS *Arizona* memorial

Quick Fact

The USS *Arizona* was named a National Historic Landmark on May 5, 1989.

What are the pros and cons of leaving the wreck of the USS *Arizona* as a memorial site? Think in terms of the environment, costs, tourism, national pride, and history.

Take Note

The USS *Arizona* holds a special place in the hearts and minds of Americans and people around the world. Its remains have been made into a memorial! Beyond the death toll, this tragedy led the U.S. into World War II. Also, the impact on the environment is still felt as it continues to leak oil.

• Do you think the USS *Arizona* should hold the top spot on our list? If you had to replace #1, which shipwreck would you choose and why?

USS ARIZONA–U.S. NAVAL HISTORICAL CENTER PHOTOGRAPH/80-G-463589; MEMORIAL AT PEARL HARBOR COURTESY OF THE PACIFIC U.S. NAVY

5   4   3   2   1

We Thought ...

Here are the criteria we used in ranking the 10 most unforgettable shipwrecks.

The shipwreck:
- Was caused by unusual or unique circumstances
- Led to tragic losses of life
- Brought changes to shipping rules and regulations
- Occurred in an unusual location
- Led us to uncharted territory
- Increased our understanding of deep-sea geography and ocean conditions
- Advanced the technology of underwater recovery
- Gave us knowledge about ancient civilizations
- Changed the course of history
- Advanced the safety standards of ships

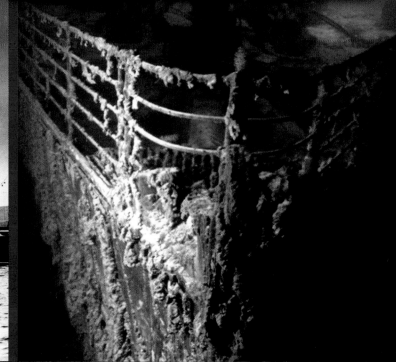

What Do You Think?

1. Do you agree with our ranking? If you don't, try ranking them yourself. Justify your ranking with data from your own research and reasoning. You may refer to our criteria, or you may want to draw up your own list of criteria.

2. Here are three other shipwrecks that we considered but in the end did not include in our top 10 list: the *Lusitania*, the *Andrea Doria*, and the *Exxon Valdez*.
   - Find out more about them. Do you think they should have made our list? Give reasons for your response.
   - Are there other shipwrecks that you think should have made our list? Explain your choices.

Index